The map

Pam is in the pit.

Dig, dig, dig.

Pam digs up a map.

Dan gets the map.

The log is on the map.

Pam digs in the mud.

Dan is sad.
Pam is not.

The map

Level 2: Story 18

Before reading

Say the sounds: g o b h e r f u l
Ensure the children use the pure sounds for the consonants without the added "uh" sound, e.g. "llll" not "luh".

Practise blending the sounds: dig log map pit mud sad gets Dan Pam digs

High-frequency words: not in on up   **Tricky words:** the is

Vocabulary check: pit – What is a sandpit? Have you ever played in one? Sandpit can be shortened to just pit. map – A drawing of a particular area with certain features identified. When have you ever seen or used a map? What is a treasure map?

Story discussion: The title and the cover illustration tell us something about the story. What do we know and what do we think might happen in this story?

Teaching points: Remind children that when they see a comma, they need to make a small pause. Practise reading the words on page 5 with appropriate pauses. Point out that in words like "digs" and "is", the letter "s" makes a /z/ sound.

After reading

Comprehension:
- What did Pam dig up in the sandpit?
- How did Dan know to go to the log?
- Why was Dan sad at the end?
- Why was Pam happy?

Fluency: Speed read the words again from the inside front cover.